YOU CAN BE A WOMAN ZOOLOGIST

Valerie Thompson
and
Judith Love Cohen

Illustrations:
David A. Katz

Editing:
Janice J. Martin

Suite 235
10734 Jefferson Blvd.
Culver City CA 90230-4969

Second Printing 1993
You Can Be a Woman Zoologist was written by Valerie Thompson and Judith Love Cohen, designed and illustrated by David Katz, and edited by Janice Martin.

This book is one of a series that emphasizes the value of science and mathematical studies by depicting real women whose careers provide inspirational role models.
Other books in the series include:
You Can Be A Woman Engineer
You Can Be A Woman Architect
You Can Be A Woman Marine Biologist
You Can Be A Woman Egyptologist
You Can Be A Woman Paleontologist

Publisher's Cataloging in Publication
(Prepared by Quality Books Inc.)

Thompson, Valerie.
You can be a woman zoologist / Valerie Thompson and Judith Love Cohen ; illustrations. David A. Katz.
p. cm.
ISBN 1-880599-08-2

1. Zoology--Vocational guidance--Juvenile literature. 2. Vocational guidance for women--Juvenile literature. I. Cohen, Judith Love. II. Katz, David A., ill. III. Title.

QL50.5.T46 1993 591'.023'082
QBI93-1092

Dedication

This book is dedicated to John Thompson for cultivating Val's appreciation of animals; to Adele Thompson for having the patience to tolerate not only her husband and daughter, but the various and sundry beasts they brought home to roost; and to Howard Siegel, who thought science was the only subject worth studying. "Woof!"

The vans bump noisily along the dirt road through the golden-bleached grass. It is technically the rainy reason, but in this part of Africa the drought has taken its toll, and the dust hangs in the air. Suddenly, a large herd of wildebeest appears over a hill, and the animals run in a seemingly endless line across the road. Valerie Thompson signals the van driver to stop.

The van passengers grab their cameras and notebooks and begin to take pictures. Valerie takes a deep breath of the scented air and laughs out loud as the wildebeest, one by one, take enormous leaps as they cross the road.

Valerie Thompson is in Africa as study leader for a group of people interested in animal behavior. The group trip, sponsored by the Zoological Society of San Diego (California), is a "dream trip" for a zoologist. Imagine spending three weeks touring the national parks in Kenya and Tanzania, studying animals and getting paid for it!

"Val, are we scaring the wildebeest?" someone asks. "No. Something else may have frightened one of the animals miles from here. When that animal galloped away, it probably set off a chain reaction, and the rest of the herd began to run in the same direction."

Valerie begins her talk about the migration of the wildebeest. Earlier that day, she told the group about elephants, and the day before, she spoke of giraffes. She looks around her. Maybe later they will see more of the wonderful birds native to Africa. She is looking forward to a future trip to Australia for more bird watching.

At times such as this, Valerie Thompson loves her job as a mammal keeper (a zoo keeper who specializes in mammals) at the San Diego Zoo. How did she get into this wonderful job? Let her tell us her story . . .

As far back as I can remember, I had an interest in animals. In fact, my family always referred to me as "the animal lover."

My grandmother had a farm in Illinois with cattle, pigs, sheep, horses and an assortment of cats and dogs. I liked spending time at the farm. I helped feed the animals and care for them. I especially liked the wild animals that lived in the area around the farm. I spent many hours looking for raccoons, muskrats, possums and wild domestic cats so that I could watch their behavior.

While I loved my days on the farm away from school, I also liked school and enjoyed most of my classes. I read books, and I liked to solve problems, the tougher the better. I was interested in most sports, and played volleyball, badminton and softball.

I also loved to visit the zoos in Chicago and watch all the animals, like the playful chimpanzees. As I watched the animals, I thought about how I would like to work at a zoo or at a wildlife park.

I always planned to go to college and study something related to living things. But it was learning about animals that meant the most to me.

In college I studied about different kinds of animals, like birds (ornithology), warm-blooded mammals (mammalogy), and cold-blooded reptiles (herpetology).

Many of the students at my college studied animal science; this could prepare them for the field of veterinary medicine. But I wanted to study and work with healthy animals doing natural things, not sick animals. I designed my own major: mostly zoology with added courses in psychology and anthropology. This major is called "animal behavior."

I began by studying biology, the study of plants, animals and microscopic living things.

Biology begins by classifying and naming things in Latin. Zoology concentrates on the animal kingdom. The animal kingdom (kingdom *Animalia*) contains groups such as worms *(Annelida)*, shellfish *(Mollusca)*, insects and spiders *(Arthropoda)*, and animals with backbones (vertebrates) such as fish, amphibians and mammals *(Chordata)*. Each of these main groups is called a phylum.

A subgroup is called a class. Among the vertebrates there are classes for fish, amphibians, reptiles, birds and mammals. Many zoologists specialize in a single class: perhaps fish (ichthyology, the study of fishes), or mammals (mammalogy, the study of animals that have hair instead of feathers).

In each class there are orders, families, genera and species. The Latin names help to describe the animals being classified.

ANIMAL
KINGDOM

I also studied about living things in general. What makes a living thing different from a rock? A living thing needs food to grow, breathes air and can create more life or have babies. Living things are made of cells, and each cell contains all the instructions for more of its kind. You, as a mammal, are made up of billions of cells. Some living things are made up of only one cell. Many cells make up tissues in animals. Many tissues make up organs in the body, such as your heart. Organs work together to make systems that permit life, such as your circulatory system. Living things are amazing and complicated! Things become even more complicated when studying why living things behave as they do.

Ethology is the study of animal behavior. It is a fascinating science that relies on the observation of animals. Animal behavior is based on two things: the set of instincts that an animal is born with, and what the animal learns from the world around it.

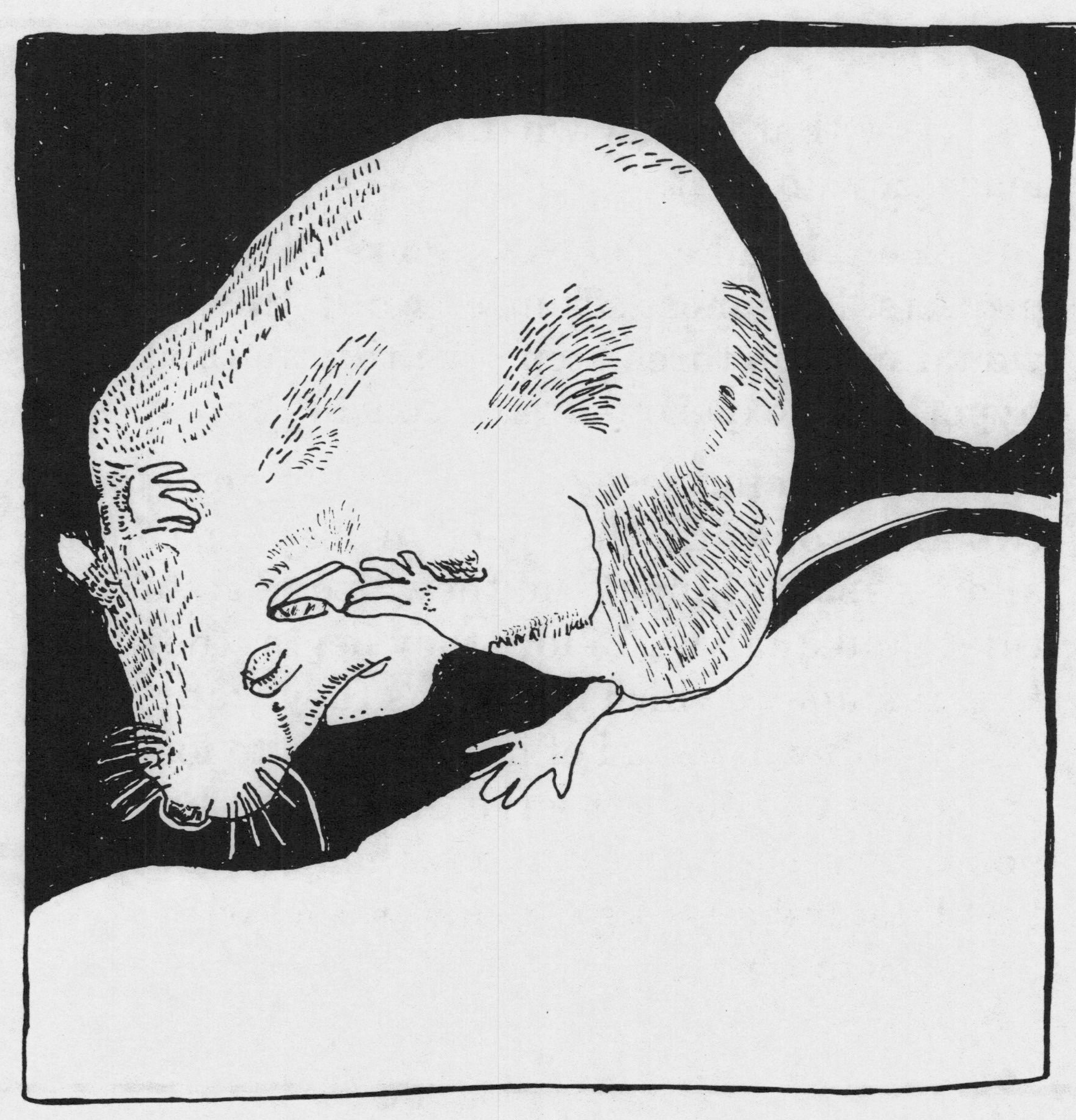

Now that I knew what zoology was, I had to learn how to do it.

Soon, I had a chance to do research projects. Like most scientific work, this research would use the three-step scientific method: hypothesis, experiment and conclusion.

When doing research, scientists need to do two kinds of work: they need to observe, count and measure things; and they also need to think and analyze. Before they begin, they need to think about which questions they want answered, what kind of information to look for, and what things to observe. After they have done their observations, they then look at all the data and analyze it to determine what the answers might be.

1.
HYPOTHESIS
2.
EXPERIMENT
3.
CONCLUSION

I chose a number of interesting topics for my research studies. In one of my early independent research project, I proposed to observe the apes in the Lincoln Park Zoo in Chicago. The zoo had recently built new exhibits for the apes, and my work would help to determine how well the apes were adapting to their new homes.

I studied the apes every day. How did they use the new space available to them? How did they behave at feeding time? How was their social behavior affected? How did the presence of the zoo visitors, now separated from the animals by only thick glass, affect the apes' behavior?

At regular intervals each day, over several weeks, I took notes on the apes' behavior. I also photographed the animals in their new homes.

Next came the painstaking task of adding up all the numbers, arriving at statistics, and graphing and analyzing the data gathered. Out of this came some exciting results. The apes used nearly all the space in their new homes, but each had favorite places to eat, sleep and play. Each ape also had different preferences for food items, much like we do. The apes also reacted to the zoo visitors. Sometimes they would pound at the glass and frighten the visitors. The amount of social behavior observed in some of the apes actually increased when the number of visitors watching increased!

Overall, these apes seemed to adjust quickly to their new homes.

Since that time I've done many studies, most recently with Queensland koalas (*Phascolarctos cinereus adustus*). We wanted to know how the koalas communicated with one another using odors produced from their scent glands. The male koalas have a scent gland on their chest that they press against trees to mark their territories. What messages are they sending? To find the answer, we observed the koalas under two conditions:

1. We watched each male's behavior when exposed to a clean, unmarked perch. We noted each time a scent mark was made and the location of each mark.

2. We watched and recorded the reaction of a second koala to the newly marked perch.

After this we summarized and analyzed the data. We tried to interpret these "scent messages" by observing the reactions of the koalas.

How can you tell if you would be good at zoology? If you can answer yes to the following questions, then you should consider becoming a zoologist.

1. Are you interested in animals? Can you respect them as the wild creatures that they are?

I always enjoy watching animals, domestic ones like dogs and cats, or wild ones like wolves or coyotes. I make sure, however, to respect them as creatures within their own domain. Some animals, like your pet dog, may jump up and down when you enter a room, but a koala is much more subtle, like a cat. I really appreciate this subtlety in my relationships with animals.

2. Do you like asking and answering questions? Are you curious?

I wanted to know how the apes that I observed adapted to their new homes, and how koalas communicate through their sense of smell.

3. Are you interested in how things work and how things are put together? Do you like to solve puzzles?

I have always liked solving tough puzzles. As a zoologist, I look for clues to solve puzzles, much like a detective. The length of an ear, the shape of a skull, the color of fur, even the structure of a cell might be the type of clue needed to identify a particular animal.

The most exciting part of my career is that there is no typical workday. One day I might work with the animals themselves, and on another day I may lead a group of visitors to the zoo and help them understand what they see. I enjoy sharing what I have learned about the animals with these zoo visitors. Younger visitors may think that they don't like science. But sometimes, after they spend a little time here, ask a question or two, and look at a few exhibits, they are suddenly quite interested in the scientific study of animals. It is rewarding to see people learn about, appreciate, and respect the animals we have here at the zoo.

I thoroughly enjoyed my job as a zoo keeper, where I had responsibility for feeding, cleaning and looking after the health of many animals. I even traveled in airplanes with some of the koalas when they were sent to other zoos so that I could ensure their safe arrival. The koalas were transported in a "sky kennel," complete with a eucalyptus perch bolted inside. The eucalyptus tree is a koala's favorite "home," and its leaves are its favorite food.

Now, as Assistant Curator of Mammals, I have much broader responsibilities which include planning the future of the zoo, its inhabitants, and its employees. We need to maintain the health and ensure the continued survival of the species as best we can. We also need to give the public good opportunities to learn about animals and assist us in our efforts to influence the conservation of our Earth's wildlife.

If you want to know things from the inside out; if you want to ask questions and understand, for example, how koalas communicate; if you are interested in how animals develop from birth to death; and if you want to help maintain nature's precarious balance by joining the fight for conservation of wildlife, then you can do it too. You can be a woman zoologist.

YOU CAN BE A WOMAN ZOOLOGIST

SCIENCE LESSON PLAN 1

PURPOSE: To gain an understanding of the behavior of animals and to learn how to go about observing this behavior.

MATERIALS: Pens, pad of paper or notebook.

PROCEDURES: Have each child select one animal to observe after school. It can be their own pet, or a neighbor's, or simply any animal that they see often.

Have the children write down what they expect to observe and when they will do it. They should observe the animals every day for a week and record the times of different behaviors seen, such as running, sleeping, swimming, barking.

Next, have the children draw a chart to illustrate some aspect of the animal's behavior. For example, a particular cat may spend between five and fifteen minutes grooming.

CONCLUSIONS: What different kinds of animals were observed?

How is the animal's behavior different from what you expected?

What were the differences in observed behavior between different types of animals? Were there differences between two of the same kind of animal?

What did you do to observe the animal without disturbing it?

SCIENCE LESSON PLAN 2

PURPOSE: To understand what special adaptations animals have.

MATERIALS: Scissors, glue, shoe boxes, art supplies (paper, crayons, paints, colored pencils, glitter, etc.).

PROCEDURES: Have children take the shoe box and create a jungle or forest inside. They should create plants, flowers, trees and animals. Animals should be shown in their proper environments: giraffes in plains, monkeys in trees, tigers in grass.

CONCLUSIONS: What are the relationships between plants, flowers and trees and the animals that depend on them? How do colors and shapes relate?

RESOURCES: Library books such as *Wildlife Encyclopedia*.

SCIENCE LESSON PLAN 3

PURPOSE: To develop a dynamic understanding of animal food webs.

MATERIALS: Spacious environment.

PROCEDURE: Have the children describe a food chain and select a different sound for each plant and animal. As a group, practice the sounds and the names of the plants or animals. Then assign the children their own specific plant or animal (more than one child can have the same plant or animal).

Have the children spread out, close their eyes and make their sounds while listening for the sounds of others. Very slowly, the children should start to take little steps and search for their own kind and the type of food they eat. When they find either one, they should hold hands and keep looking. After a period of time, call out "Stop searching," and have the children open their eyes to see the results.

CONCLUSIONS: Was it hard to find your own kind? What functions did the sounds have?

Were you captured by your predator? How could you avoid being captured?

RESOURCES: Recordings of sounds in the forest or jungle.

About the Authors:

Valerie D. Thompson is now the Assistant Curator of Mammals at the San Diego Zoo. Prior to this, she was a Lead Mammal Keeper and was involved in supporting the Zoological Society's koala education and loan program, as well as caring for the animals themselves. She received her bachelor of science degree from the University of California at Davis and her master of science degree from San Diego State University. Both degrees were in animal behavior. Valerie has done research on the Queensland koalas and a number of zoo ungulates (hooved animals), and has published numerous papers (most recently on koalas). She is active in professional organizations such as the American Association of Zoological Parks and Aquariums, the American Association of Zoo Keepers and the International Society of Zooculturists. Valerie's work has taken her to East Africa and Australia, as well as to many regions of the United States.

Judith Love Cohen is a Registered Professional Electrical Engineer with bachelor's and master's degrees in engineering from the University of Southern California and University of California at Los Angeles. She has written plays, screenplays, and newspaper articles in addition to her series of children's books that began with *You Can Be a Woman Engineer*.

About the Illustrator:

David Arthur Katz received his training in art education and holds a master's degree from the University of South Florida. He is a credentialed teacher in the Los Angeles Unified School District. His involvement in the arts has included animation, illustration, and play-, poetry- and song-writing.